Reading Essentials®
in Social Studies
COUNTRY CONNECTIONS II

UNITED KINGDOM

JOANNE MATTERN

Perfection Learning®

Editorial Director: Susan C. Thies

Editor: Mary L. Bush

Design Director: Randy Messer

Cover Design: Michael A. Aspengren

Inside Design: Michelle J. Glass, Lori Gould

IMAGE CREDITS:
Associated Press: p. 39; © Adam Woolfitt/CORBIS: p. 25; © Leif Skoogfors/CORBIS: p. 40; © Michael Boys/CORBIS: p. 33; © Ric Ergenbright/CORBIS: pp. 10, 23; © Robert Holmes/CORBIS: p. 32; © Getty Images: p. 16 (center)

Corel: cover, pp. 1, 5, 7, 8 (top), 11 (center), 14 (top), 15 (bottom), 16 (top), 17, 18 (top), 19, 20 (top), 24, 26, 28, 29, 37; Map Art: pp. 4, 9; Photos.com: back cover, pp. 2–3, 6, 8 (bottom), 11 (top), 12, 13, 14 (center, bottom), 15 (top), 16 (bottom), 18 (bottom), 20 (bottom), 21, 22, 30, 31, 34, 35, 36, 38, 41, 42, 47

TABLE OF CONTENTS

Devon, England

Just the FACTS!

Location The United Kingdom is primarily made up of four countries—England, Wales, Scotland, and Northern Ireland. England, Wales, and Scotland are on an island called Great Britain, which is located 20 miles north of France. Northern Ireland is attached to Ireland, an island west of Great Britain. The Irish Sea separates Ireland and Great Britain. Great Britain is surrounded by the Atlantic Ocean to the west, the English Channel to the south, and the North Sea to the north and east. Many small islands in these waters are also part of the United Kingdom.

Ben Nevis

Area 93,300 square miles

Geographical Features All of the countries in the United Kingdom are located on islands. Great Britain is divided into **highlands** and **lowlands**. The far northern and western areas of Great Britain feature low mountains. The southeastern coast is covered with an area of lowland, some of which lies below sea level.

Highest Elevation Ben Nevis (4409 feet above sea level)

Lowest Elevation The Fens (13 feet below sea level)

Climate Most of the United Kingdom has a **temperate** climate. Winters are mild, except in far northern parts, which can be quite cold and snowy. Much of the country receives a **moderate** amount of rainfall. In general, the western part of the country is warmer and wetter than the southern and eastern parts.

The Big Ben clock tower rises tall above the Houses of Parliament in London.

Capital City London

Largest Cities London, Birmingham, Glasgow, Liverpool, Sheffield, Leeds, Bristol, Manchester, Edinburgh

Population 60,094,648 (2003)

Languages English, Scottish Gaelic (Scotland), Welsh (Wales)

Main Religions Protestant (Anglican, Episcopal, Presbyterian), Roman Catholic

SONG FOR THE KINGDOM

"God Save the Queen" is the national anthem of the United Kingdom. This song has the same tune as the song "America (My Country Tis of Thee)." "God Save the Queen" has several verses, but the first is the one commonly sung at national events.

God save our gracious queen

Long live our noble queen

God save the queen.

Send her victorious

Happy and glorious

Long to reign over us

God save the queen!

*If a king is on the throne instead of a queen, the words are changed to "God Save the King."

Queen Elizabeth II

Government The United Kingdom is a **constitutional monarchy**. The ceremonial head of state is the king or queen. The head of the government is the prime minister.

Industries metal manufacturing, trade, electric power, shipbuilding, car and truck production, farming

Natural Resources coal, oil, natural gas, cereal grains (oats, barley, wheat), livestock, fish

Guards at Windsor Castle, the official home of the king or queen

Currency basic unit is the pound

WAVE THE UNION JACK

The United Kingdom's flag is often called the Union Jack. The red cross on the white background stands for England. The white cross on the blue background symbolizes Scotland. The red diagonal cross represents Ireland. In addition to the Union Jack, England, Scotland, and Wales have their own national flags.

CHAPTER 1

Beneath Your Feet

The United Kingdom's Land and Climate

The United Kingdom is a collection of countries and islands. England, Wales, and Scotland are located on a large island called Great Britain. Northern Ireland is on the nearby island of Ireland. These four countries in the kingdom cover approximately 93,300 square miles.

There are also many other small islands in the United Kingdom. They include the Hebrides, the Shetland Islands, the Orkney Islands, the Isle of Man, the Isle of Anglesey, and the Isle of Wight.

GEOGRAPHICAL FEATURES

The islands of the United Kingdom were once connected to the rest of Europe. When the last ice age ended about 10,000 years ago, the temperatures rose and the ice melted. The melting ice raised the level of the seas and flooded the shallow land bridge that connected Great Britain to the continent. That area is now the North Sea and the English Channel.

The United Kingdom can be divided into highlands and lowlands. The highlands are located in the northern and western areas. Scotland, Wales, and Northern Ireland are located in the highlands.

FROM SEA TO SHINING SEA

The United Kingdom is long and narrow. No part of the country is more than 62 miles from the sea.

White Cliffs of Dover on the English Channel

Although higher than the surrounding ground, no mountain in the highlands is actually very high. The highest point in the United Kingdom is Ben Nevis. Ben Nevis is located in the Grampian Mountains of Scotland. The peak is 4409 feet tall. Wales is home to the second-highest point. Mount Snowdon in the Cambrian Mountains is 3560 feet tall.

The Pennine Mountains form another important mountain chain. The Pennines are located in the northern part of England. They are sometimes called the "backbone of England" because they run down the middle of the country.

An area called the Lake District is located west of the Pennine Mountains. This area is filled with hills and lakes. The lakes were formed when glaciers scraped over the land thousands of years ago and then melted to fill in the depressions, or low areas.

Parts of northern England and Scotland are covered by moors. Moors are open areas of grasses and plants that grow close to the ground. Because these plants hold a lot of water, moors can be wet and muddy.

The southern and eastern parts of Great Britain are flat lowlands. Much of the United Kingdom's **fertile** farmland is found here. A wet **marshland** in England called The Fens contains the country's lowest point.

The United Kingdom has several important rivers and lakes. The Thames (temz) River is 210 miles long. Crossing southern England, this river flows through the city of London and empties into the North Sea.

Another important river is the Severn. The River Severn begins in North Wales and flows into England. It empties into the Bristol Channel and heads into the Atlantic Ocean.

Lough Neagh (lahk nay) is located in Northern Ireland. It is the largest freshwater lake in the United Kingdom. Most of the other large lakes in the UK are located in Scotland or England's Lake District.

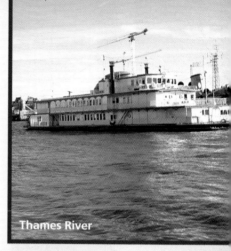

Thames River

A replica of the Loch Ness Monster

THE LOCH NESS MONSTER

Loch Ness is a lake in Scotland that is famous for being the home of the legendary sea monster called Nessie. Over the years, many people have claimed to have seen this sea monster. However, scientists have been unable to prove its existence.

CLIMATE

Most of the United Kingdom has a temperate climate. The weather is rarely very cold or very hot. Average temperatures are in the 30s during the winter and the 60s during the summer. Ocean currents from the equator bring warm air during the winter and cool breezes during the summer.

Northern parts of the country can be cold and snowy at times. However, warm air from the Gulf Stream flows over northwestern Scotland in January, making it warmer than the southern part of Great Britain. Hot, dry air from the equator sometimes blows across southern England, bringing hotter, drier conditions than in the rest of the country.

The United Kingdom is a damp, drizzly place. Storms travel across the Atlantic Ocean and dump their moisture on the British Isles. Most of the rain falls as a steady drizzle. Even when it's not raining, the sky is often cloudy. Heavy mists and **fogs** are common.

FOGGY LONDON TOWN

London used to be famous for its fogs. These fogs were especially thick about 100 years ago because homes and businesses burned coal that added smoke to the cloudy atmosphere. Today, the air is much cleaner, so the fogs aren't as thick.

CHAPTER 2

Living Wonders

The Plants and Animals of the United Kingdom

The forests, fields, and mountains of the United Kingdom provide a variety of **habitats** for plants and animals.

PLANTS

Mild temperatures and damp days create an ideal place for plant growth. The moors of the northern part of the country support a variety of short-stemmed plants and shrubs. The most common plants in this area are heather, bracken, and gorse. Heather is an evergreen plant with spiky leaves and small bell-shaped flowers of purple, pink, or white. Bracken is a type of large fern. Gorse is a spiny grayish green shrub with yellow flowers. Ferns and **rushes** can also be found in wet marshy areas.

Heather

Peat moss is found on the moors of Scotland and northern England. This moss accumulates in layers so it's easily harvested for use. In the past, peat moss provided an important source of heat. It was cut into strips, dried, and burned. Peat moss holds moisture well, so it is often mixed with drier, sandy soils to increase plant growth.

Harvested peat moss

Much of the land in the United Kingdom is covered with green forests. English oak trees grow in the central part of the country. Beechwoods are common in the south. Scotland and Wales are home to many forests filled with pine trees and other evergreens. Hardwood trees such as hawthorns and oaks are also found in Wales. Northern Ireland has forests of oak, birch, ash, hazel, and willow trees.

A variety of colorful flowers decorate the UK. Roses are common in southern England and are the country's national flower. Daffodils grow in Wales and the Lake District of England. These bright yellow flowers are the national flower of Wales. The shamrock is a leafy green plant that represents Northern Ireland. Thistle is a purple flower with prickly leaves historically used as a symbol of defense in Scotland. The Scottish bluebell, however, is the country's national flower.

Shamrocks

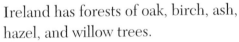

As an island country, the United Kingdom has miles of coastline. Sea campions, sea spurreys, and sea pinks are just a few of the plants that grow along the coastal shores and cliffs. Plants that grow near the sea must be able to survive the salty spray that constantly washes over them. Many seacoast rocks are covered with tough red campions and gray, green, or yellow organisms called *lichens*.

Lichens

> **A LOT OF MOWING TO DO**
>
> One hundred and fifty different types of grass grow in the United Kingdom.

ANIMALS

Mammals At one time, large **predators** such as wolves, bears, and wild boars lived in the United Kingdom. These animals were hunted so heavily, however, that they no longer live there. Wildcats are very rare and can only be found in **remote** areas of Scotland.

Today, the largest animal in the United Kingdom is the deer. Scotland and England's Lake District are home to the red deer. Red deer are large deer with reddish brown summer coats that turn grayish brown in the winter. Woodlands in the western part of the UK are home to smaller roe deer. Fallow deer live in most parts of England. These deer vary in color, and the males have impressive antlers that they shed and regrow each year.

Red deer

Shetland pony

Several wild and **domestic** horse breeds are **native** to the United Kingdom. Wild ponies roam the moors of southwestern England. Wild Welsh ponies are sturdy horses that continue to thrive in the hills and mountains of Wales. Shetland ponies are miniature horses from Scotland. These small horses are only about three feet tall. They were originally bred to pull carts in coal mines. Today, they are popular pets for children. Clydesdales are huge horses from Scotland. These horses stand five to six feet tall and were first used for pulling farm equipment.

Many smaller mammals make their homes in the UK. Foxes, hedgehogs, squirrels, rabbits, badgers, and mice can be found in a variety of habitats across the country. Bats used to roost in old barns and abandoned buildings. However, most of these buildings have been torn down, so these flying mammals are becoming endangered. The countryside is an ideal environment for otters, voles, and stoats. The polecat is found in wooded areas of Wales. Scotland and Northern Ireland are home to the pine marten.

Vole

Otter

Seals inhabit some of the smaller islands and other coastal areas of the United Kingdom. More than half of the grey seals in the world live in the waters of the British Isles. These seals can dive to depths of 230 feet and stay underwater for more than 30 minutes. They eat fish from the sea.

Birds Small birds fill the skies of the British Isles. Robins, warblers, and thrushes are a few common songbirds in the country. Woodpeckers and nuthatches climb trees in search of insects and nuts.

Larger birds of **prey** are found in more **rural** areas. The ptarmigan and the peregrine falcon fly over the Scottish highlands searching for smaller birds and mammals to eat. Red kites glide overhead in Wales. Golden eagles soar through the skies of Scotland and the Hebrides Islands.

Peregrine falcon

Seagulls, hawks, ducks, and geese live near the coast, where they can find fish and other prey in the water. Gannets can be seen off the coasts of Scotland and Wales. These large seabirds have wingspans of up to six feet. Gannets often plunge quickly into the sea to grab unsuspecting fish.

BIRD LAND

The Orkney Islands are sometimes called the "bird islands." Many visitors come to watch the millions of birds that make their home on these islands.

Reptiles and Amphibians   Many reptiles and amphibians live in the woods and gardens of the United Kingdom. The most common are frogs, newts, lizards, and nonpoisonous snakes. All amphibians and reptiles are protected by law in the United Kingdom. It is illegal to hunt, kill, or harm these animals.

Fish   The waters around the British Isles are full of fish and other **marine** life. Herring, halibut, plaice, pollack, and cod swim in the Atlantic waters. Shellfish, such as shrimp, crabs, and lobsters, are plentiful.

Freshwater rivers and lakes in the country are full of fish too. A variety of trout and salmon provide food and sport for many people.

Trout

CHAPTER 3

Looking Back
The United Kingdom's History

THE BEGINNING OF THE KINGDOM

The United Kingdom's first people came from northwestern Europe about 10,000 years ago. These people lived in simple huts. They raised cattle and planted crops. They also made pottery and carved stone.

HENGES AND BARROWS

The ancient Britons built many stone circles called *henges*. The most famous of these circles is Stonehenge. Stonehenge is on the Salisbury Plain in southern England. Huge stones from Wales are arranged in two circles. Stonehenge still stands today, and thousands of tourists visit it every year.

The ancient people also left barrows in southern England. Barrows are long burial mounds. Archaeologists have found ancient treasures, such as cups, jewelry, and daggers, in these barrows.

Stonehenge

A group of people called the Celts (kelts) arrived in the United Kingdom around 700 B.C. They came from the central part of Europe. The Celts found gold, copper, and tin in mines around Great Britain. They used these minerals to make weapons, tools, coins, and jewelry. They also introduced iron to the British Isles.

Hadrian's Wall

In 43 A.D., the Roman emperor sent an army to conquer the British people. The Romans built forts and roads across Great Britain. In 122 A.D., Emperor Hadrian built a stone wall to mark the northern edge of the Roman **empire**. Hadrian's Wall still stands today. It is near the present-day border between England and Scotland.

The Romans called Scotland's natives Picts. *Picts* means "painted" in Latin. The Picts painted their bodies with bright colors. They wore their hair long and decorated themselves with jewelry. The Picts were fierce fighters who kept the Romans from ever conquering Scotland and its people.

Roman soldiers remained in the United Kingdom until the 400s. Then they were called back to Rome because of trouble at home. After the Romans left, the UK was invaded by a series of tribes from Europe, including the Jutes, Angles, and Saxons from Germany and Denmark. These tribes drove the Celts north into Scotland and west into Wales. In time, the Anglo-Saxons became the rulers of what is now England.

Roman soldiers storm Great Britain by sea.

During the 800s, the United Kingdom was attacked by Viking raiders from Norway. The Vikings took over parts of England. For many years, bitter fighting between the Vikings and the Anglo-Saxons tore the country apart. Finally, in 886, the Anglo-Saxon king Alfred the Great drove the Vikings out of most of the kingdom. Viking settlements remained in the eastern part of England for another 200 years.

THE NORMAN INVASION

In 1066, Harold was the Anglo-Saxon king of England. A man named William of Normandy believed that he had the right to be Great Britain's king. He invaded southern England and defeated King Harold at the Battle of Hastings on October 14, 1066. William became King William I of England.

The Normans built castles and forts to control the British people. They also created new towns and marketplaces all over the country. William gave his followers large areas of land. Gradually, British society became more like that of France and other parts of Europe.

> **NOTES ON NORMANDY**
>
> For many years, England and France fought for control of Normandy, an area of land located near the English Channel. Today, Normandy is a region in France. It was the site of the famous World War II D-Day Invasion, which was launched by the United States in an attempt to end the war.

King William I in battle

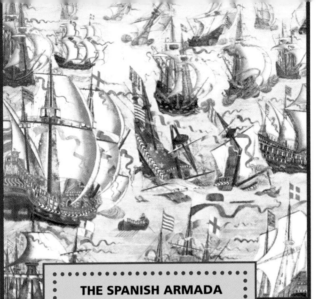

A POWERFUL EMPIRE

As the centuries passed, England became one of the most powerful countries in the world. Her explorers traveled the globe. They claimed faraway lands in the name of the king or queen of England. England's army and navy grew strong too. England fought and won several battles against France and Spain.

UNITING THE KINGDOM

Although Wales and England were both ruled by the Normans, Wales struggled to become an independent country. During the 1100s, part of northern Wales became independent and had its own king. England, however, wanted to control all of Wales. In 1272, the Welsh king Llywelyn ap Gruffudd refused to accept Edward I of England as king. Edward invaded Wales in 1277 and defeated Llywelyn five years later. In 1284, all of Wales fell under the control of the English king.

In 1603, Queen Elizabeth I of England died. She had never married or had children. However, she was related to James, who was the king of Scotland. When Elizabeth died, James became the king of both England and Scotland. For the first time, the two countries were united. However, many Scots continued to fight for their independence for many years to come.

Ireland also struggled with England for control of its land. For centuries, terrible battles were fought between the two nations. England tried to force its **culture** and laws on Ireland. It also tried to change Ireland's religion. Many people in Ireland were Catholic. However, England officially followed the Protestant religion. During the 1600s, England passed laws that took away the rights of Irish Catholics.

In 1918, Ireland set up a separate government. For the next two years, much fighting took place between Irish and English soldiers. Many innocent people were killed. This time became known as "The Troubles." Finally, in 1920, Ireland split into two countries. Most of Ireland became an independent country, but the six northern counties remained under British control and became known as Northern Ireland. Troubles between Great Britain and Northern Ireland continue even today.

> **MORE TROUBLES**
>
> Another period of "Troubles" occurred from 1960 through the 1990s. Protests and violence between Northern Ireland and Great Britain increased. In 1998, the Stormont Treaty was signed by Ireland, Great Britain, and Northern Ireland. Great Britain promised peace in exchange for Ireland giving up all claims to Northern Ireland and Northern Ireland gaining more say in the government. Despite the agreement, fighting has continued among all parties.

Northern Ireland

THE RISE AND FALL OF THE BRITISH EMPIRE

Between 1837 and 1901, Queen Victoria ruled Great Britain. This period was known as the Victorian era. It was a time of British prosperity and power. At that time, Great Britain ruled countries all over the world. Her empire included Canada, Australia, Egypt, India, and many other countries. It was said that "the sun never set on the British empire" because it covered so much of the world.

Great Britain fought in World War I (1914–1918) and World War II (1939–1945). During World War II, parts of the United Kingdom were bombed by Germany. After the war, the country faced years of **economic** struggles.

During this time, the British empire began to shrink. Many countries became independent. The United Kingdom remained an important nation, but it would never again be as powerful as it had been during the late 1800s.

THE UNITED KINGDOM TODAY

Today, Great Britain is a constitutional monarchy. The government is run by a prime minister and a group of lawmakers called the Parliament. The Parliament is divided into two houses—the House of Commons and the House of Lords. Members of the House of Lords are appointed by birth just as kings and queens are. Members of the House of Commons are elected by the people. Scotland, Wales, and Northern Ireland all send representatives to the British Parliament.

THE ROYAL FAMILY

The royal family has been an important part of British society for centuries. For many years, the king or queen truly was the leader of the nation. Today, the king or queen is still the ceremonial head of the government, but he or she has little real power. However, the royal family remains important to the United Kingdom and its culture.

Scotland also has its own parliament. However, this government body cannot control taxes or sign treaties with other countries. It is only in charge of local laws, education, and environmental issues.

The British people have a great deal of personal freedom. Civil rights and equality among the races have become important in recent years. All citizens over the age of 18 have the right to vote, and many Britons are active in shaping their government and their country.

Each autumn, the queen travels to the House of Lords in England to open the new parliamentary session.

CHAPTER 4

Digging In to the United Kingdom's
Resources and Industries

The United Kingdom has a wealth of natural energy resources. The country's **economy** is based mainly on manufacturing and other industrial efforts. However, agriculture remains an important source of jobs and food.

Battersea Power Station in London

SOURCES OF ENERGY

The most abundant mineral in the UK is coal. For centuries, coal mines have provided a major source of income for people in South Wales, northeast and central England, and parts of Scotland. Coal was once the major source of heat and energy for the United Kingdom's homes and factories. However, in recent years, oil and other sources of energy have replaced coal, which creates a lot of pollution when it's burned. Experts believe there is enough coal to last the country for another 200 years. However, it is too expensive to remove this coal from the ground. As a result, many miners have lost their jobs.

Oil and natural gas have become important energy sources for the UK over the past 40 years. Oil and natural gas were discovered under the North Sea during the 1960s. Today, many oil and gas rigs remove these underwater resources.

Scotland and Wales use **hydroelectricity**. This source is limited in other parts of the UK where there's a lack of fast-moving water to run hydroelectric plants.

In addition, a few nuclear power plants provide energy for the country. Nuclear power involves splitting the particles of certain materials to release energy. It doesn't use up natural resources or create much waste. However, the power plants are expensive to build and operate and the process can be dangerous, so many British citizens don't support this type of energy production.

MANUFACTURING, SERVICES, AND TRADE

Manufacturing is largely responsible for the United Kingdom's strong economy. Metals, machine tools, vehicles, ships, and airplanes are major industries.

In recent years, the UK has become more active in manufacturing electronics. Scotland is a major producer of computers. Many **biotechnology** firms are located in the English cities of Oxford, Cambridge, Manchester, and Leeds. British factories also manufacture **fiber optics** equipment, robots, and other hi-tech products.

The service industry employs more people than any other industry in the United Kingdom. Service industries include shopping, banking, tourism, and transportation. For centuries, London has been one of the world's most important cities in banking and insurance.

Trade is important to the United Kingdom's economy. The nation's most important **exports** are machines, chemicals, clothing, cars, ships, farm machinery, medicines, and electronics equipment. The country **imports** cotton, rubber, sulfur, and about half of its food products.

The United Kingdom is a member of the European Union. The Union is an organization of many European countries. Its goal is to make it easier for countries to trade with one another and use one another's products.

> **THE POUND VERSUS THE EURO**
>
> Most countries in the European Union use a unit of currency called the *euro*. However, so far the United Kingdom has refused to use the euro. Instead, it continues to use the pound.

AGRICULTURE

British agriculture provides more than half of the country's food needs. Almost 75 percent of the United Kingdom's land is used for farming or grazing. Most of the land in eastern and southern England, as well as eastern Scotland, is used to grow crops. Oats, barley, wheat, potatoes, and sugar beets are the country's top crops. Northern areas provide excellent grazing land for cattle and sheep.

FISHING

Most **commercial** fishing is done off the coasts of Scotland and southwestern England. Fish are also raised on farms throughout the country. Although the United Kingdom is a nation of islands, fishing provides a surprisingly small amount of its food. The UK actually imports more fish than it exports. Fishing employs less than one percent of the British people.

CRAZY COWS AND OTHER PROBLEMS

During the 1990s, some British cattle became sick with a brain disorder called *mad cow disease*. Millions of animals were destroyed, and people in the United States and Europe refused to buy or eat British beef.

In 2001, foot-and-mouth disease affected British sheep and livestock. Again, millions of animals had to be destroyed, and people stopped eating meat from British animals.

The British farming industry is still recovering from these events.

OLD MACDONALD HAD A FISH

Fish farms are businesses that raise fish to sell as a food product. Most fish farms are rivers or lakes where people control the conditions so fish can multiply quickly.

CHAPTER 5

The Many Faces of the United Kingdom

Discovering the United Kingdom's People

Approximately 60 million people live in the United Kingdom. Most of these people live in England. Scotland has a population of just over 5 million people. About 3 million people live in Wales, while about 1.6 million make their homes in Northern Ireland. Much smaller populations inhabit the many islands that are part of the country.

LIFE IN THE CITIES

At one time, most people in the United Kingdom lived in rural areas. Today, however, almost 90 percent live in **urban** areas.

London is the largest city in the UK. It is also the largest city in Europe. About 7 million people live in London. Many more **commute** to jobs in the city from outlying areas.

London

Like many British cities, London is a mix of the old and the new. Castles and Victorian **row houses** stand near modern high-rise buildings. The streets are crowded with

The Tube

people, cars, and buses. An underground train called the Tube rumbles below the streets.

Other British cities are major industrial centers. Numerous factories, plants, offices, and docks are found in the cities of Liverpool, Birmingham, Manchester, Glasgow, and Belfast. Many industrial cities have suffered from unemployment. However, some areas have continued to prosper. For example, Manchester and Leeds have thriving computer and information technology industries that have brought these cities back to life.

Double-decker bus

Most city residents live in apartments or small houses. Apartments are called *flats*. Houses are often connected to one another in rows. These living arrangements allow a large number of people to live in crowded areas.

Cities in the United Kingdom also have poor areas called *slums*. Slums are often crowded and unsafe. Over the past 30 years, the British government has built many new housing units for slum dwellers. These houses are sometimes called "council houses" because they are built and owned by the city council. These housing units provide improved living conditions for many people.

LIFE IN THE COUNTRY

Today only a small percent of the United Kingdom's people live in rural areas. Some of these people farm the land or raise livestock. Others live in the country but commute to office jobs in the city.

Rural residents often live in small houses. Some have thatched roofs made of grass and straw. Other houses are made of stone or brick.

Living in the country provides fresh air and open space. However, it can be difficult to get services to people who live far apart from one another. Some stores and services have mobile units that travel from house to house. Other rural residents travel to nearby villages and cities to shop, find medical care, and meet with friends.

Scotland's countryside

CHAPTER 6

A Slice of Life

British Culture

The culture of the United Kingdom is a diverse blend of four distinct countries, each with its own style and traditions.

FOOD

Traditional British food is plain and filling. Beef, lamb, eggs, potatoes, bread, and vegetables are basic **staples** of the British diet. Cheese and dairy products round out meals. Fish and chips is a popular British meal. Chips are deep-fried potatoes like American French fries. Yorkshire pudding is *not* a yummy British dessert. Instead, it is a type of biscuit that is usually served with roast beef.

Haggis is a traditional Scottish dish. Chopped-up pieces of a sheep's heart, lungs, and liver are stuffed into the sheep's stomach lining and boiled. Porridge and kippers are Scottish breakfast foods. Porridge is made by cooking oatmeal with salt, sugar, and milk. Kippers are smoked herrings.

A Scottish butcher displays haggis.

Most British people drink tea with their meals. "Tea" is also the name given to a late afternoon snack of tea, small sandwiches, and biscuits (cookies). "Cream tea" includes scones, or biscuits, topped with jam and thick cream. "High tea" is a tasty British tradition that includes a variety of sandwiches, pastries, rolls, and cookies—all served with tea, of course!

In recent years, many people from India, Pakistan, Africa, and the Middle East have moved to the UK. These people brought their own food traditions to Great Britain. Indian food, such as the spicy meat dish called *curry*, is served in many homes and restaurants.

WELSH RAREBIT

Welsh rarebit is a Wales specialty. It is similar to an open grilled cheese sandwich.

ingredients

3 ounces grated cheddar cheese

1 tablespoon milk

1 tablespoon butter

1 teaspoon mustard powder

dash of salt

dash of cayenne pepper

dash of Worcestershire sauce

2 slices of bread

directions

1. Mix the first seven ingredients together in a bowl.

2. Toast the bread lightly.

3. Place the bread on a metal tray. Spread the cheese mixture on top. Place in a toaster oven or broiler until the cheese melts and browns slightly on top.

CLOTHING

Most people in the United Kingdom dress the same way as people in the United States or western Europe. **Immigrants**, however, sometimes wear traditional clothing. It is not unusual to see Indian women wearing long dresses called *saris*. Muslim men often wear white robes and head coverings. Some Muslim women cover their bodies with long dark dresses and veils.

The kilt is a traditional item of clothing worn by men in Scotland. This knee-length skirt is worn with a belt that holds a leather pouch called a *sporran*. A kilt has a plaid pattern that symbolizes one of the Scottish **clans**.

EDUCATION

All children in the United Kingdom must go to school until they are 16 years old. Most children start school at age five. In Northern Ireland, children start school when they are four. The government provides free education for children through a system of state schools. More than 90 percent of children in the UK attend state schools. Others go to private schools, where they pay for their education.

When they are 16, students take a series of exams called GCSEs. GCSE stands for "general certificate of secondary education." Students must take exams in each subject they study. Passing the GCSEs is similar to earning a high school diploma.

Students who want to go on to college must pass a different set of exams. These students stay in school until they are 18 years old. Then they can go on to a university.

More than 90 universities are located in the United Kingdom. Some, such as Oxford and Cambridge, have been around for hundreds of years. Other schools specialize in sciences, technical trades, or art. More than half of British students go on to a university. Those who don't usually study a trade or go to work.

SPORTS AND LEISURE ACTIVITIES

Sports are a pastime for many players and fans in the United Kingdom. The most popular sport is football. British football is similar to American soccer. Most major cities have their own football teams, and fans are famous for their loyalty. Many Britons play rugby, which is similar to American football. Cricket is another British team sport. In this game, players use a bat to try to "bowl" a ball through their opponent's **wicket**.

The Highland Games are held in Scotland every year. These games feature foot races, dancing, and traditional Scottish games like tossing the caber (a long wooden pole).

People all over the United Kingdom enjoy cycling, hiking, skiing, fishing, and playing tennis. American sports, such as baseball and American football, are also growing in popularity.

PUTTING AROUND SCOTLAND

Golf was invented in Scotland. Today, a Scottish golf course called Saint Andrews is one of the most impressive courses in the world.

London Ferris wheel

Outdoor activities allow people to enjoy the mild weather of the UK. Many Britons spend time in national or local parks. Seaside resorts in England and Wales are crowded in the summer. Thousands of people vacation at beaches, amusement parks, and shopping areas in seaside towns.

Pubs are an important gathering place in cities and towns all over the UK. *Pub* is short for "public house." A pub serves food and drinks and provides entertainment for its customers.

RELIGION

The Church of England is the official church of the United Kingdom. Scotland also has its own official church called the Church of Scotland. Both of these churches are Protestant.

Hundreds of years ago, there was no freedom of religion in the UK. A person had to belong to the Church of England, and other religions were against the law. Today, the British people are free to worship as they please. Large Jewish and Catholic communities exist along with the many Protestant groups.

CHURCH OF THE KING

The Church of England was started by King Henry VIII during the 1500s. King Henry was angry when the Catholic Church wouldn't allow him to divorce his first wife to marry another woman. So King Henry broke away from the Catholic Church and formed the Church of England.

As more people from Pakistan, India, and the Middle East move to the United Kingdom, the Muslim religion has continued to grow. Today there are about 1.5 million Muslims in the UK. Communities have built their own mosques, or houses of worship.

HOLIDAYS

People in the United Kingdom celebrate national and religious holidays. Families gather to celebrate Easter, Christmas, and New Year's Day. The day after Christmas is also a holiday in Great Britain. December 26 is Boxing Day. In the past, servants received gifts from their employers on this day. Today, gifts are given to mail carriers, garbage collectors, and other service providers.

Guy Fawkes Day is celebrated on November 5. In 1605, Guy Fawkes tried to blow up the Houses of Parliament. He was captured and killed. This event is celebrated with large bonfires and fireworks.

On March 1, people in Wales celebrate St. David's Day. St. David is the **patron saint** of Wales. On this day, Welsh people wear leeks (a vegetable similar to an onion) on their coats as a symbol of their country.

Houses of Parliament

ARTS

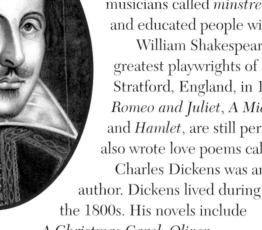

The United Kingdom has a long tradition of art, literature, and theater. In ancient times, traveling musicians called *minstrels* and *bards* entertained and educated people with songs and stories.

William Shakespeare is considered one of the greatest playwrights of all time. He was born in Stratford, England, in 1564. His plays, such as *Romeo and Juliet*, *A Midsummer Night's Dream*, and *Hamlet*, are still performed today. Shakespeare also wrote love poems called *sonnets*.

Charles Dickens was another very popular British author. Dickens lived during the 1800s. His novels include *A Christmas Carol*, *Oliver Twist*, and *Great Expectations*.

William Shakespeare

His work often showed how miserable life was for poor people in Great Britain during the Victorian era.

Scotland has had its share of famous authors as well. Robert Louis Stevenson wrote adventure novels and children's poetry. Sir Walter Scott entertained millions with historical adventures like *Ivanhoe*. More recently, millions of readers have enjoyed J. K. Rowling's tales of the young wizard Harry Potter.

Charles Dickens

Many writers from the United Kingdom are known for their poetry. Seamus Heaney was born in Northern Ireland. Dylan Thomas wrote poetry about life in Wales. Robert Burns wrote poems in his native Scottish **dialect** and is recognized as Scotland's national poet.

WHO WROTE WHAT?

Below are other British writers and their works.

- Jane Austen wrote *Pride and Prejudice*.
- H. G. Wells wrote the science fiction classics *The War of the Worlds* and *The Time Machine*.
- Sir Arthur Conan Doyle created the famous detective Sherlock Holmes.
- The Brontë sisters wrote romantic novels such as *Jane Eyre* and *Wuthering Heights*.
- J. R. R. Tolkien created the fantasy world of *The Hobbit* and *The Lord of the Rings*.

The British Isles have given the world many skilled artists and designers as well. Artists Joshua Reynolds and Thomas Gainsborough painted unforgettable portraits. J. M. W. Turner and John Constable painted British landscapes. Barbara Hepworth and Henry Moore are famous for their sculptures. Laura Ashley, a designer whose flower prints became popular on dresses and home furnishings during the 1970s and 1980s, was born in Wales.

Many talented musicians come from the UK. The Beatles were natives of Liverpool, England. Other popular British musicians include singers Elton John (England) and Charlotte Church (Wales), the rock band U2 (Northern Ireland), and theatrical composer Andrew Lloyd Webber (England).

The Beatles on *The Ed Sullivan Show*

CHAPTER 7

What's Ahead?

A Look at the United Kingdom's Future

Integrating four individual countries into one has been a challenge for the United Kingdom. The diverse people, cultures, and beliefs have sometimes clashed, but over time, the UK has remained strong. Overcoming current issues will help the nation maintain its stability.

Catholic Irish Republican Army supporters attack a British patrol unit in Northern Ireland.

UNITY OR DIVISION?

The United Kingdom is not really united. For centuries, people in Scotland, Wales, and Northern Ireland have fought to free themselves from English rule. Wales and Scotland desire independence from the UK, but they rely on Britain's economy too much. Great Britain, in turn, needs those countries' products to support its economy. In recent years, disputes over religion and **politics** have led to terrible violence in Northern Ireland. Religious, political, and economic differences need to be resolved among the countries to keep the Kingdom truly united.

ECONOMIC TROUBLES

In the past several decades, the UK has faced economic troubles. Many industries have closed or reduced their need for workers. This has resulted in many citizens losing their jobs.

The government has spent large sums of money to help poor people and communities. It offers free health care to all residents. Unemployment benefits and low-cost housing also help struggling people. However, these programs cost the government millions of dollars each year. In the future, communities in the UK will need to find new ways to provide jobs and services for their people in order to improve the national economy.

DISCRIMINATION AND IMMIGRATION

In the past 40 years, many different **ethnic** and racial groups have immigrated to the United Kingdom. Introducing new cultures has often caused tension and violence. African Americans, Asians, and Middle Easterners face **discrimination**. Many live in poor areas and cannot find good jobs or housing. Meanwhile, some Britons don't like the presence of people from other cultures in their country. Incidents of violence among racial groups continue.

Every year, many people enter the United Kingdom illegally to find work and better living conditions. This has become a serious social and economic problem, especially in the cities. Large numbers of these immigrants cause further crowding in areas where a shortage of space, food, shelter, and jobs already exists.

Indians are the largest minority group in the United Kingdom.

THE ENVIRONMENT

The United Kingdom is a small country with a fairly large population. There is great concern that the natural environment is disappearing under a wave of housing developments, highways, shopping malls, and high-rise office buildings. Animals have become endangered because their habitats have disappeared. The government and local environmental groups are trying to preserve the land by creating more national parks. The National Parks Authority has been given the charge of protecting the land, plants, and wild animals of the UK.

The UK also wants to keep the environment clean and safe. Both the government and private citizens are fighting to clean up polluted rivers, reduce the amount of air pollution, and find cleaner sources of energy.

PLEASE DON'T PICK THE FLOWERS

Many species of wildflowers and other plants are protected by law in the United Kingdom. That means you can look (and smell) but you'd better not touch!

LOOKING FORWARD

The United Kingdom has a rich history of royalty and influence in the world. The country has weathered many changes, and there is much hope for the future of this proud nation.

England's countryside

INTERNET CONNECTIONS AND
RELATED READING FOR THE UNITED KINGDOM

Just the Facts!
http://www.enchantedlearning.com/europe/britain/index.shtml
Find out more interesting facts about the UK, its countries, its flag, and its land.

http://www.factmonster.com/ipka/A0108078.html
Learn "monstrous" facts about the UK at this site.

Chapter 1
http://1uptravel.com/international/europe/united-kingdom/topography.html
This travel site features information about the United Kingdom's climate and geography.

http://moors.uk.net/
Want to know more about the moors of Scotland? Then visit this North York Moors National Park Web site.

Chapter 2
http://www.uksafari.com/wildfiles.htm
Go on a United Kingdom safari and see the unique animals and plants that make their home there.

http://www.mammal.org.uk/facts.htm
Use these fact sheets to brush up on your knowledge of mammals in the UK.

http://www.fishing-in-wales.com/wildlife/index.htm
Follow this "guide to the wildlife of Wales" to discover the plants and animals of the country.

Chapter 3
http://www.stonepages.com
Read these "Stone Pages" for more information on historical stone structures in England, Ireland, Scotland, and Wales.

http://www.bbc.co.uk/history/forkids/
Explore the United Kingdom's history with the games, puzzles, timelines, stories, facts, and other activities at this historical site for kids.

http://www.explore.parliament.uk
Packed with information on Parliament, this site includes a virtual tour and information on how the British government works.

http://www.royal.gov.uk/output/Page1.asp
This is the official Web site of the royal family. Make sure to check out the "kids' zone."

Chapter 4
http://www.mbendi.co.za/indy/ming/eu/uk/p0005.htm
This brief overview of the mining industry includes links to specific minerals produced in the country as well as other industries in the United Kingdom.

Chapter 5

http://www.toweroflondontour.com/kids/
Tour the city of London with Reginald the Raven. See all the hot spots on this kid-friendly trip through Britain' largest city.

http://www.enchantedlearning.com/school/Britain/
Check out some famous faces (explorers, scientists, and inventors) of Britain.

Chapter 6

http://www.oxfam.org.uk/coolplanet/ontheline/explore/journey/uk/ukindex.htm
Take a virtual culture journey through the UK. Experience the nation's foods, sports, music, arts, and more.

http://www.1uptravel.com/international/europe/united-kingdom/locallife.html
Learn more about life in the United Kingdom with this overview of the people, languages, and religions. Click on "cuisine," "holidays," and "festivals" for a glance of those aspects of British life.

http://www.nationalgallery.org.uk/
Tour the National Gallery for an online look at British works of art.

Chapter 7

http://news.bbc.co.uk/cbbcnews/
This special BBC (British Broadcasting Corporation) Web site is a current events site specially designed for students.

○ ○ ○ ○ ○ ○ ○ ○ ○ ○ ○ ○ ○ ○

Diana, Princess of Wales by Kristine Brennan. A Women of Achievement title. Chelsea House, 1999. [RL 3 IL 3–6] (5512801 PB)

Dropping In On England by Lewis K. Parker. A title in the Dropping In On series. Rourke Book Company, Inc., 1994. [RL 5.5 IL 3–8] (5877706 HB)

England by Jean F. Balshfied. An Enchantment of the World book. Children's Press, 1997. [RL 7 IL 5–9] (3731006 HB)

England by Michael Burgan. This book is a basic overview of the history, geography, climate, and culture of England. Children's Press, 1999. [RL 3.8 IL 3–5] (6861406 HB)

Shakespeare and Me by Cynthia Mercati. Rosalind disguises herself as a boy in order to join a group of traveling actors who are performing with William Shakespeare at the Globe Theatre in London. Perfection Learning Corporation, 2001. [RL 2.9 IL 4–8] (3173901 PB 3173902 CC)

•RL = Reading Level
•IL = Interest Level
Perfection Learning's catalog numbers are included for your ordering convenience. PB indicates paperback. CC indicates Cover Craft. HB indicates hardback.

GLOSSARY

iotechnology   (beye oh tek NAHL uh gee) process of using living organisms to manufacture materials such as foods and medicines

lan   (klan) group of families descended from a common ancestor

ommercial   (kuh MER shuhl) related to the buying and selling of goods

ommute   (kuh MYOUT) to travel to work or school each day

onstitutional monarchy   (kahn stuh TOO shun uhl MAH nar kee) system of government that has a king or queen as the head of the state but is run by a prime minister and governing body

ulture   (KUHL cher) beliefs, customs, and social activities of a country or group of people

ialect   (DEYE uh lekt) regional variety of a language

iscrimination   (di skrim uh NAY shuhn) unfair treatment of a person or group, usually because of race, ethnic group, age, religion, or gender (see separate entry for *ethnic*)

omestic   (doh MES tik) type of animal raised as a pet or farm animal

conomic   (ek uh NAH mik) relating to the economy of a country (see separate entry for *economy*)

conomy   (ee KON uh mee) country's system of making, buying, and selling goods and services

mpire   (EM peyer) group of countries that has the same ruler

thnic   (ETH nik) relating to a group that shares a common culture (see separate entry for *culture*)

export	(EKS port) product sent to another country to sell
fertile	(FER tuhl) good for growing
fiber optics	(FEYE ber OP tiks) system of transferring information through a number of thin, flexible glass or plastic tubes
fog	(fawg) clouds of moisture hanging in the air at or near ground level; clouds of any substance, such as water vapor or smoke
habitat	(HAB i tat) place where a plant or animal lives
highland	(HEYE land) area of hilly or mountainous land
hydroelectricity	(heye droh i lek TRIS uh tee) electricity made from energy produced by running water
immigrant	(IM uh gruhnt) person who moves to one country from another country
import	(IM port) to buy products from another country
lowland	(LOH land) area of land that is flatter or lower than the surrounding land
marine	(muh REEN) having to do with the ocean or sea
marshland	(MARSH land) area of lowland often covered by water (see separate entry for *lowland*)
moderate	(MAH der uht) not extremely large or small
native	(NAY tiv) originally living or growing in an area
patron saint	(PAY trin saynt) holy person who is believed to look after a country
politics	(PAHL uh tiks) policies and activities of the government
predator	(PRED uh ter) animal that hunts other animals for food

ey   (pray) animal that is hunted by other animals for food

mote   (ree MOHT) isolated; far away from people

w house   (roh house) house that is joined to others by its side walls

ral   (ROOR uhl) having to do with life in the country

sh   (ruhsh) marsh plant with tubelike stems and leaves that look like blades of grass

aple   (STAY puhl) main food in the diet of a group of people

mperate   (TEMP ruht) having temperatures that are neither too hot nor too cold

rban   (ER bin) having to do with life in the city

icket   (WIK it) three stumps topped by two crosspieces at which the ball is bowled in cricket

INDEX